Practical Pre-School Books

Match your theme to the EYFS

Planning for Learning through Dinosaurs

by Marianne Sargent. Illustrated by Cathy Hughes

Contents

Published by Practical Pre-School Books, A Division of MA Education Ltd,
St Jude's Church, Dulwich Road, Herne Hill, London, SE24 0PB Tel: 020 7738 5454

www.practicalpreschoolbooks.com

Planning for Learning through Dinosaurs ISBN: 978-1-909280-74-8

Making plans

Child-friendly planning

The purpose of planning is to make sure that all children enjoy a broad and balanced experience of learning. Planning should be flexible, useful and child-friendly. It should reflect opportunities available both indoors and outside. Plans form part of a planning cycle in which practitioners make observations, assess and plan.

Children benefit from reflective planning that takes into account the children's current interests and abilities and also allows them to take the next steps in their learning. Plans should make provision for activities that promote learning and a desire to imagine, observe, communicate, experiment, investigate and create.

Plans should include a variety of types of activity. Some will be adult-initiated or adult-led and focus on key skills or concepts. This should be balanced with opportunities for child-initiated activity where the children take a key role in the planning. In addition, there is a need to plan for the on-going continuous provision areas such as construction, sand and water, malleable materials, small world, listening area, book corner, role-play and mark-making. Thought also needs to be given to the enhanced provision whereby an extra resource or change may enable further exploration, development and learning.

Furthermore, the outdoor environment provides valuable opportunities for children's learning. It is vital that plans value the use of outdoor space.

The UK Frameworks

Within the UK a number of frameworks exist to outline the provision that children should be entitled to receive. Whilst a variety of terms and labels are used to describe the areas of learning there are key principles which are common to each document. For example, they advocate that practitioners' planning should be personal, based on observations and knowledge of the specific children within a setting. They also acknowledge that young children learn best when there is scope for child-initiated activity. In addition, it is accepted that young children's learning is holistic and although areas of learning are presented separately within each framework, in reality children's activities and explorations cross over and combine the different subject areas. Thus the areas of learning are perhaps of most use for planning, assessment and recording to ensure that key areas are not overlooked.

Focused area plans

The plans you make for each day will outline areas of continuous provision and focused, adult-led activities. Plans for focused activities need to include aspects such as:

- resources needed;
- the way in which you might introduce activities;
- individual needs;
- the organisation of adult help;
- size of the group;
- timing;
- safety;
- key vocabulary;
- key questions.

Identify the learning and the Early Learning Goals that each activity is intended to promote. Make a note of any

Making plans

assessments or observations that you are likely to carry out. After carrying out the activities, make notes on your plans to say what was particularly successful or any changes you would make next time.

A final note

Planning should be seen as flexible. Not all groups meet every day, and not all children attend every day. Any part of the plan can be used independently, stretched over a longer period or condensed to meet the needs of any group. You will almost certainly adapt the activities as children respond to them in different ways and bring their own ideas, interests and questions. The important thing is to ensure that the children are provided with a varied and enjoyable curriculum that meets their individual developing needs.

Using the book

Read the section which outlines links to the Early Learning Goals (pages 4-6) and explains the rationale for focusing on 'Dinosaurs'.

The chart on page 7 gives an example format for weekly planning, including on-going continuous provision as well as more focused activities.

Use pages 8 to 19 to select from a wide range of themed, focused activities that recognise the importance of involving children in practical activities and giving them opportunities to follow their own interests. For each 'Dinosaur' theme, two activities are described in detail as examples to help you in your planning and preparation. Key vocabulary, questions and learning opportunities are identified. Use the activities as a basis to:

- Extend current and emerging interests and capabilities
- Engage in sustained conversations
- Stimulate new interests and skills.

Find out on page 20 how the 'Dinosaur' theme can be brought together by creating a prehistoric play landscape.

Use page 21 for ideas of resources to collect or prepare. Remember that the books listed are only suggestions. It is likely that you will already have within your setting a variety of other books that will be equally useful.

The activity overview chart on page 23 can be used either at the planning stage or after each theme has been completed. It will help you to see at a glance which aspects of children's development are being addressed and alert you to the areas which may need greater input in the future.

As children take part in the activities, their learning will progress. 'Collecting evidence' on page 22 explains how you might monitor each child's achievements.

There is additional material to support the working partnership of families and children in the form of a reproducible Family Page found inside the back cover.

It is important to appreciate that the ideas presented in this book will only be a part of your planning. Many activities that will be taking place as routine in your group may not be mentioned. For example, it is assumed that sand, dough, water, puzzles, role play, floor toys, technology and large scale apparatus are part of the ongoing early years experience. Role-play areas, stories, rhymes, singing and group discussion times are similarly assumed to be happening each week although they may not be a focus for described activities.

Using the 'Early Learning Goals'

The principles that are common to each of the United Kingdom curriculum frameworks for the early years are described on page 2. It is vital that, when planning for children within a setting, practitioners are familiar with the relevant framework's content and organisation for areas of learning. Regardless however, of whether a child attends a setting in England, Northern Ireland, Scotland or Wales they have a right to provision for all areas of learning. The children should experience activities which encourage them to develop their communication and language; personal, social, emotional, physical, mathematical and creative skills. They should have opportunities within literacy and be encouraged to understand and explore their world.

Within the Statutory Framework for the Early Years Foundation Stage (2014), Communication and Language; Physical Development and Personal, Social and Emotional Development are described as Prime Areas of Learning that are 'particularly crucial for igniting children's curiosity and enthusiasm for learning, and for building their capacity to learn, form relationships and thrive' (page 7, DfE 2014). The Specific Areas of Learning are Literacy, Mathematics, Understanding the World and Expressive Arts and Design. For each area of learning the Early Learning Goals (ELGs) describe what children are expected to be able to do by the time they enter Year 1. These goals, detailed on pages 4 to 6, have been used throughout this book to show how the activities relating to 'Dinosaurs' aim to help children meet these expectations. For example, for Personal, Social and Emotional Development, one aspect relates to the development of children's 'self-confidence and self-awareness'. Activities aimed at helping children develop in this area have the reference PSE1. This will enable you to see which of the Early Learning Goals are covered for a given theme and to plan for areas to be revisited and developed.

In addition, an activity may be carried out to develop a range of areas of learning. For example, when the children make Pterosaur mobiles they will develop skills in art and design as well as their fine motor skills, which are part of physical development. Thus, whilst focused adult-led activities may have clearly defined goals at the planning stage, it must be remembered that as children take on ideas and initiate their own learning and activities, goals may change.

The Prime Areas of Learning

Communication and Language

Listening and attention: children listen attentively in a range of situations. They listen to stories, accurately anticipating key events and respond to what they hear with relevant comments, questions or actions. They give their attention to what others say and respond appropriately, while engaged in another activity. (CL1)

Understanding: children follow instructions involving several ideas or actions. They answer 'how' and 'why' questions about their experiences and in response to stories or events. (CL2)

Speaking: children express themselves effectively, showing awareness of listeners' needs. They use past, present and future forms accurately when talking about events that have happened or are to happen in the future. They develop their own narratives and explanations by connecting ideas or events. (CL3)

'Dinosaurs' activities provide many opportunities for children to enjoy listening, understanding and speaking. By playing the word games with dinosaur names, children are encouraged to count syllables and listen for initial sounds. They also talk about their favourite dinosaurs, examine toys and describe their features. Children find out about volcanoes by watching videos and looking up information in books, prompting them to ask questions, talk and share ideas. In addition, as role-play archaeologists they engage in conversation that is rich in topical language, expanding their vocabulary.

Physical Development

Moving and handling: children show good control and coordination in large and small movements. They move confidently in a range of ways, safely negotiating space. They handle equipment and tools effectively, including pencils for writing. (PD1)

Health and self-care: children know the importance for good health of physical exercise, and a healthy diet, and talk about ways to keep healthy and safe. They manage their own basic hygiene and personal needs successfully, including dressing and going to the toilet independently. (PD2)

'Dinosaurs' activities offer many opportunities for children to enjoy movement activities and handle tools and equipment. Whilst excavating dinosaur fossils and building large and small-scale models out of modelling and construction materials they practice fine motor control. They also improve their gross motor skills and coordination when moving like dinosaurs and going on a dinosaur hunt over rough and physically demanding terrain.

Furthermore, when looking at the difference between herbivores and carnivores, children find out what it means to be vegetarian or vegan and how such diets need to be balanced carefully so as not to impact upon health.

Personal, Social and Emotional Development

Self-confidence and self-awareness: children are confident to try new activities, and say why they like some activities more than others. They are confident to speak in a familiar group, will talk about their ideas, and will choose the resources they need for their chosen activities. They say when they do or don't need help. (PSE1)

Managing feelings and behaviour: children talk about how they and others show feelings, talk about their own and others' behaviour, and its consequences, and know that some behaviour is unacceptable. They work as part of a group or class, and understand and follow the rules. They adjust their behaviour to different situations, and take changes of routine in their stride. (PSE2)

Making relationships: children play cooperatively, taking turns with others. They take account of one another's ideas about how to organise their activity. They show sensitivity to others' needs and feelings, and form positive relationships with adults and other children. (PSE3)

It is possible to use 'Dinosaurs' as a gateway theme through which to explore personal, social and emotional issues. For example, by reading *Gigantosaurus* by Jonny Duddle in Theme 1, the children learn about the risks involved in crying wolf one too many times. Jane Yolan's *How Do Dinosaurs...* series explores a range of subjects and one such book is used in Theme 2 to look at table manners at snack time. Also *Romp in the Swamp* by Ian Whybrow is used as inspiration for working together and collaborating to create a small world dinosaur swamp in Theme 4.

Many aspects of Personal, Social and Emotional Development will be covered on an almost incidental basis. Any activity that involves making choices or showing initiative will promote self-confidence and self-awareness. There are also many dinosaur–themed games on the market that encourage turn taking and cooperation, as well as puzzles that children can complete together.

The Specific Areas of Learning

Literacy

Reading: children read and understand simple sentences. They use phonic knowledge to decode regular words and read them aloud accurately. They also read some common irregular words. They demonstrate understanding when talking with others about what they have read. (L1)

Writing: children use their phonic knowledge to write words in ways which match their spoken sounds. They also write some irregular common words. They write simple sentences which can be read by themselves and others. Some words are spelt correctly and others are phonetically plausible. (L2)

'Dinosaurs' is an exciting theme and there are a great many picture books on the market featuring interesting stories and brilliant artwork. Having access to such a great selection helps practitioners to get children, and especially boys, excited about stories and reading. For example, in Theme 3 *Can I Bring My Pterodactyl to School, Ms Johnson?* by Lois G Grambling is used to inspire the children to make up their own story events. Also, by reading books such as Claire Freedman's *Dinosaurs Love Underpants* in Theme 6, children are exposed to rhythmical, rhyming and alliterative texts that help to develop their awareness of sounds in language. Children then suggest their own vocabulary to describe how dinosaurs moved in Theme 2 and build a word bank to describe what happens when a volcano erupts in Theme 6.

Using non-fiction titles with high quality illustrations to find out interesting facts draws the children in and gets them wanting to learn more. In Theme 1 children use information about carnivorous dinosaurs to make vital statistics posters and in Theme 5 they find out about extinction theories.

Furthermore, the role-play archaeological dig and museum in Theme 6 provide purposeful early writing opportunities including making signs, writing information labels and recording notes and observations about prehistoric finds.

Mathematics

Numbers: children count reliably with numbers from 1 to 20, place them in order and say which number is one more or one less than a given number. Using quantities and objects, they add and subtract two single-digit numbers and count on or back to find the answer. They solve problems, including doubling, halving and sharing. (M1)

Shape, space and measures: children use everyday language to talk about size, weight, capacity, position, distance, time and money to compare quantities and objects and to solve problems. They recognise, create and describe patterns. They explore characteristics of everyday objects and shapes and use mathematical language to describe them. (M2)

There are plenty of 'Dinosaurs' activities that aim to help children develop their knowledge of numbers. Children count teeth, bones and footprints and sing counting rhymes such as 'Ten Dancing Dinosaurs'. They create pictograms and learn how to use them to find out which is the least or most scary of the carnivorous dinosaurs. Children also explore different aspects of shape, space and measure as they examine the size and scale of these enormous reptiles. What's more, volcanoes offer the perfect opportunity to explore capacity as children fill and empty bottles with red lava water.

Understanding the World

People and communities: children talk about past and present events in their own lives and in the lives of family members. They know that other children don't always enjoy the same things, and are sensitive to this. They know about similarities and differences between themselves and others, and among families, communities and traditions. (UW1)

The world: children know about similarities and differences in relation to places, objects, materials and living things. They talk about the features of their own immediate environment and how environments might vary from one another. They make observations of animals and plants and explain why some things occur, and talk about changes. (UW2)

Technology: children recognise that a range of technology is used in places such as homes and schools. They select and use technology for particular purposes. (UW3)

'Dinosaurs' is a great hands-on outdoor topic that presents many opportunities for learning about the natural world. Children look closely at dinosaurs' physical features and sort and classify them into herbivores, carnivores, land, sky and marine species. In Theme 6 they pretend to be archaeologists and excavate their natural environment. They learn about fossilisation and how scientists can use the information and evidence they find to learn about the past. In the concluding activity, children find out what the prehistoric landscape was like and consider different extinction theories. In doing so they take a closer look at volcanoes and the impact an eruption could have on people living nearby. All the time they are using factual books and the Internet to gather information and find out more.

Expressive Arts and Design

Exploring and using media and materials: children sing songs, make music and dance, and experiment with ways of changing them. They safely use and explore a variety of materials, tools and techniques, experimenting with colour, design, texture, form and function. (EAD1)

Being imaginative: children use what they have learnt about media and materials in original ways, thinking about uses and purposes. They represent their own ideas, thoughts and feelings through design and technology, art, music, dance, role-play and stories. (EAD2)

Children explore a wide variety of materials, tools and techniques as they make Pterosaur mobiles, prehistoric play landscapes and models of dinosaurs, as well as painting pictures, making collages and creating murals. They use their imaginations to think about what dinosaurs might have sounded like and how the different creatures moved. Furthermore, in Theme 2, children read books such as *Bumpus Jumpus Dinosaurumpus!* by Tony Mitton and use them as inspiration for dance and music. They can also use instruments to recreate the sound of a volcano erupting.

Note

The Early Learning Goals raise awareness of key aspects within any child's development for each area of learning. It is important to remember that these goals are reached through a combination of adult and child-initiated activities within early years settings as well as in the child's home. Thus, it is vital that goals are shared by practitioners and parents, and children are given every opportunity to develop throughout their Early Years Foundation Stage both in their setting and at home.

Example chart to aid planning in the EYFS

Week beginning:	Monday	Tuesday	Wednesday	Thursday	Friday
FOCUSED ACTIVITIES					
Focus Activity 1:					
Focus Activity 2:					
Stories and rhymes					
CONTINUOUS PROVISION (Indoor)					
Collage					
Construction (large)					
Construction (small)					
ICT					
Imaginative play					
Listening					
Malleable materials					
Mark making					
Painting					
Role play					
Sand (damp)					
Sand (dry)					
Water					
CONTINUOUS PROVISION (Outdoor)					
Construction					
Creative play					
Exploratory play					
Gross motor					
ENHANCED PROVISION (Indoor)					
ENHANCED PROVISION (Outdoor)					

Theme 1: Meat-eating predators

Communication and Language

- Play dinosaur name games. Say the names of different dinosaurs out loud and clap the syllables. Challenge the children to think of an alliterative name for each dinosaur. The name must start with the same **sound** as the species, for example Anna Ankylosaurus or Daniel Diplodocus. (CL1, 2, 3)
- Press some giant dinosaur footprints into the sand pit or soil area. Otherwise print some muddy footprints running through the setting. Upturn tables and chairs as if something has come crashing through in the night. Stand back and let the children speculate about what has happened. (CL1, 2, 3)

Physical Development

- Take the children to a large space and encourage them to move like enormous dinosaur predators. For example, Velociraptor (running fast), Pterodon (swooping), Gigantosaurus (stomping), Tylosaurus (swimming and leaping out of the water), Troodon (running together in packs). (PD1)
- Make dinosaurs out of construction materials, such as brio, Lego, stickle bricks or magnetic blocks. (PD1)

Personal, Social and Emotional Development

- Read *Gigantosaurus* by Jonny Duddle. It is a story about a little dinosaur who cries wolf one too many times. Talk about little Bonehead's antics and ask the children why his friends stopped believing him. Ask them why Bonehead was lucky. What could have happened? (PSE2)

Literacy

- Recite the rhyme, 'I Had a Tiny T-rex' (see activity opposite). (L1)
- Make vital statistic posters for the fiercest carnivorous dinosaurs. Invite the children to draw or paint large pictures of dinosaurs. Use information books to find out how tall, heavy, strong and fast each dinosaur was. Look up how many spikes, claws or teeth they had. Find out how many millions of years ago they existed. Write these facts on the posters. (L1, 2)

Mathematics

- Make a pictogram of scariest meat-eating dinosaurs (see activity opposite). (M1, 2)
- Print off some pictures of carnivorous dinosaurs with mouths wide-open. Count how many teeth each dinosaur has. (M1)
- Use playground chalk to draw numbered dinosaur footprints on the floor outside for the children to jump on. (M1)
- Read *Ten Terrible Dinosaurs* by Paul Stickland. Line up ten toy dinosaurs in a row and take away one each time. (M1)

Understanding the World

- Use information books and the Internet to find out what dinosaurs were. Ask the children if they have seen or touched any reptiles that are alive today. Can they describe what a reptile feels like to touch? Arrange for someone to bring some reptiles into the setting for the children to see. (UW2)
- Explain the difference between herbivores and carnivores using animals and reptiles as examples. Find out what different dinosaurs ate. Look at how their physical features helped them source and eat different types of food, for example, Tyrannosaurus' large teeth for ripping into meat and Brachiosaurus' long neck for reaching high branches. (UW2)

Expressive Arts and Design

- Make fierce carnivorous dinosaur masks with big sharp teeth and dress up like dinosaurs. (EAD1)
- Make junk model dinosaurs. (EAD1)

- Read *Katie and the Dinosaurs* by James Mayhew. Ask the children to imagine going on a similar adventure. Which dinosaur would they like to go with? Where would they go and what would they do? (EAD2)

Activity: I Had a Tiny T-rex

Learning opportunity: Shows awareness of rhyme and alliteration; joins in with repeated refrains and anticipates key phrases in rhymes.

Early Learning Goal: Literacy. Reading.

Resources: Water tray; soapy water; Tyrannosaurus rex toys; water aprons

Key vocabulary: Bubble, bubbly, frothy, pop, dip, splash, swim, paddle.

Organisation: Small group

What to do: Give each child a toy Tyrannosaurus rex. Encourage them to join in the following rhyme, which is based on the traditional version about a turtle:

I had a tiny T-rex, his name was Tiny Tim,
I put him in the bath tub to see if he could swim.
He drank up all the water and gobbled up all the soap,
Then when he tried to talk he had bubbles in this throat.
Bubble, bubble, bubble, bubble… pop!

As you recite the rhyme, swim the toy dinosaurs in the water. When singing the last line drop the dinosaurs in the water, raise hands into the air and clap them for the pop.

After singing the rhyme allow the children time to play around with the bubbly water and encourage them to talk about how it looks, feels and sounds.

Activity: Dinosaur pictogram

Learning opportunity: Counts reliably with numbers from one to 20; uses everyday language to compare quantities.

Early Learning Goal: Mathematics. Numbers. Shape, space and measure.

Resources: Playground chalks; tub of sorting dinosaurs.

Key vocabulary: Numbers to twenty, names of dinosaurs, count, how many, total, altogether, column, pictogram, most popular, least popular.

Organisation: Whole group.

What to do: Use playground chalks to draw a grid on the floor outside. Write numbers to 10 down one axis and place a selection of toy dinosaurs from a sorting tub along the other axis.

Invite the children to choose what they believe to be the scariest of the meat-eating dinosaurs from the tub and place it on the grid in the corresponding column.

Encourage the children to look for data presented in the graph by asking them questions. Can they see which is the most scary/least scary of the meat-eating dinosaurs? Can they count how many thought each dinosaur was scariest? Can they work out how many children voted altogether? Can they think of any other ideas for pictograms?

Display

Set up an interactive carnivore/herbivore sorting display. Put two hoops on a table, one labelled 'carnivore', with a picture of some meat next to it, and another labelled 'herbivore', with a picture of a plant. Place a bowl full of toy dinosaurs in between the hoops. Display pictures and posters of various dinosaurs eating to help the children decide.

Theme 2: Gentle giants

Communication and Language

- Bring a small group of children together to examine a selection of toy herbivorous dinosaurs that have distinctive features. For example, Stegosaurus (plates on its back), Triceratops (three horns), Brachiosaurus (long neck) and Ankylosaurus (bumpy armour). Hide the dinosaurs. Choose one at a time and put them in a feely bag. Invite the children to take turns at feeling and describing the different dinosaurs whole the other children guess what is in the bag. (CL1, 2)
- Invite individual children to come to the front and tell the group which is their favourite dinosaur and why. (CL3)
- Play dinosaur rescue (see activity opposite). (CL1, 2)

Physical Development

- Read *Linus the Vegetarian T-Rex* by Robert Neubecker. Talk about vegetarian diets. Find out if any of the children in the group are vegetarian or if their parents are. Can the children explain what 'vegetarian' means? Talk about the different reasons behind vegetarianism. Explain what a vegan is. (PD2)
- Cook a vegetarian meal. Talk about the health benefits of eating a wide range of vegetables. Explain how vegetarians replace the protein they would otherwise get from meat by using pulses, nuts, seeds, eggs and meat substitutes. (PD2)

Personal, Social and Emotional Development

- Read *How Do Dinosaurs Eat Their Food?* by Jane Yolen and Mark Teague. It takes a humorous look at good table manners. This is a good book to share at snack or lunchtime. (PSE2)

Literacy

- Read books such as *Dinosaur Dig, Dinosaur Rescue* or *Dinosaur Zoom* by Penny Dale to explore rhyming onomatopoeic vocabulary. (L1)
- Sound out and write some onomatopoeic words that describe dinosaur movements, for example, thud, thump, trod, stamp. (L2)

Mathematics

- Recite 'Ten Dancing Dinosaurs' from *Dinosaur Poems* by Korky Paul. Encourage the children to hold up ten fingers, folding them down as the rhyme progresses. (M1)
- Use toy dinosaurs to make sets of footprints in the sand tray. Count the prints. Use pairs of prints to count in twos. Work out the total number of prints. Using the size and shape of the different footprints, figure out how many dinosaurs might have made them. (M1)
- Make a Brachiosaurus height chart. Draw the dinosaur on a large piece of paper and invite the children to paint it. Draw a measuring scale up the Brachiosaurus' neck. Bring the children to the chart and mark their heights on the scale. Compare the heights and about who is the tallest/shortest. (M2)

Understanding the World

- Look at a selection of herbivorous dinosaurs, examine their individual characteristics. Use information books to find out what purpose these features served. (UW2)
- Make dinosaur cookies. (UW2)
- Create giant dinosaur silhouettes (see activity opposite). (UW2)
- Find out why the Brontosaurus ate stones. (UW2)

Expressive Arts and Design

- Read *The Dance of the Dinosaurs* by Colin and Jacqui Hawkins or *Bumpus Jumpus Dinosaurumpus!* by Tony Mitton and Guy Parker-Rees. Take the children to a wide open space either indoors or outside, read the rhyming

onomatopoeic text aloud and encourage everyone to dance like the dinosaurs. Introduce drums, tambourines and shakers for the children to play as they dance. (EAD1)

Activity: Dinosaur rescue

Learning opportunity: Listens attentively and follows directions; follows instructions involving several ideas or actions.

Early Learning Goal: Communication and Language. Listening and attention. Understanding.

Resources: Small toy herbivorous dinosaurs and a large carnivorous dinosaur.

Key vocabulary: On, under, above, below, next to, beside, alongside, toward, behind, in front, indoors, outside.

Organisation: Small groups.

What to do: Hide herbivorous dinosaurs all over the setting. Gather four children and divide them into two pairs. Set some ground rules before the start of the game; the children must take care not to pull or push each other during the search.

Give one pair a large carnivorous dinosaur and tell them to make it roar. Explain that the other pair are going to be the plant-eating dinosaurs' rescuers. The children must listen carefully to your instructions and find the plant-eating dinosaurs. The aim of the game is for the pair of rescuers to find the hiding dinosaurs before the pair with the meat-eating dinosaur does.

Allow the pairs to take turns being the rescuers.

Activity: Giant dinosaur silhouettes

Learning opportunity: Talks about why things happen and how things work.

Early Learning Goal: Understanding the World. The world.

Resources: Lamp with bright bulb; large white sheet; pegs; washing line or rope; large table; toy dinosaurs.

Key vocabulary: Silhouette, bigger, smaller, light, shadow, shine, bright, bulb, behind, project.

Organisation: Small groups.

What to do: Fix a washing line or rope so that it stretches across a room. Peg a white sheet onto the washing line. Place a large table behind the sheet and set up a lamp with a bright bulb so that it is shining at the table and towards the sheet. Then darken the room so that the lamp is the only light source.

Invite the children to bring toy dinosaurs to the table and set up a scene. The take them around to the other side of the sheet where they will see a silhouette of the scene. The dinosaurs will be magnified in size.

Encourage the children to move the dinosaurs around on the table to see if they appear bigger or smaller in the silhouette.

Safety note: Take care when using lamps. Ensure the children are fully aware of the dangers of touching a hot bulb.

Display

Create a *Dinosaurs Galore* display based on the book by Giles Andreae and David Wojtowycz. Invite the children to paint pictures of the different dinosaurs featured in the book. Type out the verses in a large font and display them surrounded by the children's paintings.

Theme 3: Dinosaurs in the sky

Communication and Language

- Read *The Super Swooper Dinosaur* by Martin Waddell and Leonie Ward. During the story pause to ask why each of the games are unsuitable for the Pterosaur . Do the children have any ideas about games they could play with a Pterosaur ? (CL1, 2, 3)
- Show the children pictures of Pterosaurs. Can they imagine what noises each Pterosaur made? Do they think the noise would be quieter/louder, higher/lower in bigger/smaller Pterosaurs? Look at the size and shape of crests on the Pterosaur heads. How do the children think the crest would affect the sounds? Encourage them to use a wide range of vocabulary to describe the sounds. (CL1, 2, 3)

Physical Development

- Make a Pterosaur mobile (see activity below). (PD1)
- Encourage children to jump off low apparatus and swoop like Pterosaurs. (PD1)

Personal, Social and Emotional Development

- Read *William Worrydactyl* by Brian Moses and Mike Gordon. Talk about the story with the children. Do they ever feel like William? Is there anything they could do to help make themselves feel better? (PSE1, 2)

Literacy

- Write out some Pterosaur species names. Talk about how strange and long the words are. Read them out slowly, break them into syllables and count the number of letters. (L1)
- Read *Can I Bring My Pterodactyl to School, Ms Johnson?* by Lois G Grambling and Judy Love. Ask the children what might happen if they brought a real Pterosaur into the setting. How might it be useful? What about other dinosaurs?(L1)

Mathematics

- Make ten Pterosaur shaped number cards, punch holes in them and hook them onto a washing line for number activities. (M1)
- Cut 2D shapes out of card and encourage the children to make Pterosaur pictures with them. Can the children explain why they have used certain shapes for different parts of the Pterosaurs' bodies? (M2)

Understanding the World

- Visit the BBC Nature website to access some 'Walking with Dinosaurs' videos. Explain to the children that scientists and film-makers have created computer-generated images of how they think dinosaurs looked, moved and sounded. Find out how the Rhamphorhynchus flew low in the sky, skimming the water for fish and how the Ornithocheirus glided on air currents to cross the ocean. (UW2, 3)
- Make Pterosaur kites. Take them out and fly them on a windy day. (UW2)

Expressive Arts and Design

- Provide plastic coat hangers and a variety of craft materials for the children to experiment with creating Pterosaur mobiles of their own design (see activity below). (EAD1)
- Make some 'dinosaur' eggs for the children to discover (see activity opposite). (EAD1)

Activity: Pterosaur mobile

Learning opportunity: Handle tools, objects and construction materials safely and with increasing control.

Early Learning Goal: Physical Development. Moving and handling.

Resources: Wire coat hangers; thick cardboard; card; scissors; string; thread; stapler; pencils; paint.

Key vocabulary: Pterosaur, fly, wings, wing-span, soar, float, high, air, hang, join, tie, cut, draw, slot.

Organisation: Small groups.

What to do: Draw several outlines of Pterosaur bodies and wings on thick card. Cut these out for use as stencils.

Give the children some card and a body and wing stencil each. Help them to draw around the stencils and cut the shapes out. Let them paint their dinosaurs and add any features they wish.

When the dinosaur pieces are dry, cut a horizontal slot into the centre of the body piece and feed the wings through.

Slot two wire coat hangers together so that they make a criss-cross shape and fix them in place with string. Tie a length of thread to each protruding end and attach to the Pterosaurs.

Activity: Dinosaur eggs

Learning opportunity: Beginning to make believe by pretending.

Early Learning Goal: Expressive Arts and Design.
Being imaginative.

Resources: Plaster of Paris; squeezy bottle; funnel; plastic jug; large spoon; balloons; balloon pump; sharp scissors; tray filled with water; acrylic paints and brushes.

Key vocabulary: Egg, crack, buried, nest, size, big, large.

Organisation: Whole group.

What to do: Use Plaster of Paris to make some 'dinosaur' eggs and leave them in the outdoor area for the children to discover.

Pour two cups of Plaster of Paris through a funnel into a squeezy bottle. Add one cup of water and shake the bottle until completely mixed and lump free. Fit a balloon over the bottle neck and pour the plaster mix in. Use a balloon pump to blow up the balloon. Tie the balloon and roll it around so that the plaster coats the entire inside. Keep rolling the balloon around until you can no longer feel any plaster moving inside. Float the balloon in a tray of water to prevent it from loosing its shape. Repeat several more times and leave for 24 hours to set.

Gently cut the balloons away from the plaster eggs with sharp scissors or a craft knife and paint them with acrylic paint. They are quite delicate but it doesn't matter if any break because you can make it look as though they are hatching.

Make a mud nest and arrange the eggs inside it for the children to discover.

Stand back and let them talk between themselves about what they have found. Listen to what they say and extend their thinking by making your own observational comments, such as, 'I wonder what type of creature could have laid eggs like those'.

Extend this activity by helping the children make their own dinosaur eggs.

Another idea is to make more robust solid eggs out of clay and bury them in the sand pit or soil area for the children to discover. (Many Pterosaurs buried their eggs.)

Display

Create a Pterosaur diorama. Cut the lid off a large cardboard box and turn it on its side. Invite the children to paint the inside of the box sky blue and add clouds using cotton wool or tissue paper. Provide art and craft resources and allow the children to make some model Pterosaurs using whatever methods and materials they choose. Use thread to hang the Pterosaurs from the top of the diorama so they look as though they are flying through the air.

Theme 4: Dinosaurs of the deep

Communication and Language

- Examine a selection of dinosaur toys including those that dwelled in the sea, sky and on land. Ask the children to describe the different features of each dinosaur. Encourage the children to use descriptive vocabulary to talk about how each dinosaur would have moved. (CL1, 2, 3)
- Make dinosaur ice eggs. Put small toy dinosaurs inside water balloons. Fill the balloons with water and freeze. Peel the balloons off and put the eggs in the water tray for the children to examine. Encourage them to talk about how the eggs feel and what the dinosaurs look like inside. Can the children explain how the ice eggs were created and what is happening to them now? (CL2, 3).

Physical Development

- Provide a waterproof polymer modelling clay (such as Fimo) for the children to make some marine dinosaurs. Once baked and cooled the dinosaurs can be played with in the water tray. (PD1)

Personal, Social and Emotional Development

- Read *Romp in the Swamp* by Ian Whybrow and Adrian Reynolds (see activity below). (PSE1, 2, 3)

Literacy

- Sing *Row, row, row, your boat gently down the steam, if you see a Plesiosaur don't forget to scream!* Try different variations with other dinosaurs, for example: *Fly, fly, fly your plane swiftly through the sky, if you see a Pterosaur don't forget to cry!* Or *Stamp, stamp, stamp your feet on the jungle floor, if you see Triceratops don't forget to roar!* Ask the children if they have any other suggestions. (L1)

Mathematics

- Set out some containers numbered one to 10 next to the water tray. Fill the tray with marine dinosaurs. Provide nets for the children to fish them out and fill the tubs with the correct number. (M1)
- Find out exactly how big a marine dinosaur was (see activity opposite). (M2)

Understanding the World

- Use information books to find out about dinosaurs that lived in the sea. (UW2)
- Investigate water resistance. Look at how marine dinosaurs moved through the water using large flippers. Fill a deep water tray and provide a variety of objects for the children to experiment with, including tennis rackets, spatulas, sieves and flippers. Talk about how easy or difficult it is to drag each object through the water. Encourage the children to try it with their hands; with their fingers closed and spread apart. Can they say which is easier and why? (UW2)

Expressive Arts and Design

- Make a boat out of a large cardboard box and place it on top of some blue sheets and blankets outside. Provide a large piece of netting, waterproofs, wellies, fishing nets, rope and binoculars for the children to pretend they are dinosaur hunters at sea. (EAD2)

Activity: Romp in the swamp

Learning opportunity: Play cooperatively, taking account of one another's ideas; talk about ideas and choose the resources they need; talk about how they and others show feelings.

Early Learning Goal: Personal, Social and Emotional Development. Making relationships. Self-confidence and self-awareness. Managing feelings and behaviour.

Resources: Romp in the Swamp; water tray; toy dinosaurs; water aprons; access to water toys and equipment.

Key vocabulary: Swamp, water, wet, soaked, dance, play, romp, together, fun, friends.

Organisation: Small groups.

What to do: Read *Romp in the Swamp* to the children. Talk about how Harry is feeling when he arrives at Charlie's house. Consider whether he might be feeling shy about playing with someone new. Think about why Harry is reluctant to share his dinosaurs.

At the end of the story help the children reflect upon what happened when Harry joined in and decided to share his toys. Talk about how much fun the children and the dinosaurs all had.

Invite the children to play together as a group and create a dinosaur swamp in the water tray outside. Encourage them to come up with ideas and independently seek out the materials and resources they need.

Activity: How big were they really?

Learning opportunity: Use everyday language to talk about and compare size.

Early Learning Goal: Mathematics. Shape, space and measure.

Resources: Playground chalks; measuring tapes; information books about marine dinosaurs; digital camera.

Key vocabulary: Measure, size, length, height, long, short, tall, wide, longer, shorter, bigger, smaller, massive, enormous, biggest, smallest.

Organisation: Small groups

What to do: Use information books to find out how big some marine dinosaurs were. Take the children out into a large open tarmacked space. Ask a child to use playground chalk to draw around you on the floor. Measure the length of your 'human' outline and write it alongside.

Draw some rough dinosaur outlines in the remaining space. The children can help by holding the tape measure as you mark out the length. You can also direct them to stand as place markers as you draw. Write the dinosaur lengths next to the outlines.

Stand back and look at the images. Invite the children to think of words to describe the size of the dinosaurs. Read out the measurements. Talk about which is biggest/smallest, longest/shortest.

Ask the children to lie down next to the images. Stand on a stepladder or chair and take some photos from above. Use the photos to encourage further discussion later.

Tip: Prepare by drawing an outline of each dinosaur on a piece of paper beforehand. Most information books have diagrams comparing the size of a dinosaur to the size of a human. These are a good guide.

Display

Make a large-scale collage. Draw out an outline of a marine dinosaur on a large display board that the children can reach. Mark on some basic details, such as skin markings, flippers and eyes. Invite the children to collage with crepe paper, taking care to choose colours that create patterns and highlight features. Provide blue and green tissue paper and cellophane to create a watery effect and cover the rest of the board. Allow the children to choose additional different craft materials if they want. Encourage them to talk about their choices and if they have any other ideas to enhance the collage.

Theme 5: Explosive landscape

Communication and Language

- Upload the sound of a volcanic eruption from the Internet onto an MP3 player and hide it somewhere in the setting. Challenge the children to listen and search out where the sound is coming from. (CL1)
- Show the children a diagram of what happens in a volcanic eruption. Watch some video footage and encourage the children to explain what is happening. (CL2, 3)

Physical Development

- Create a prehistoric landscape for the children to navigate as dinosaur explorers (see activity opposite). (PD1)
- Mould volcano shapes in wet sand and sprinkle on red and orange coloured sand for lava. (PD1)

Personal, Social and Emotional Development

- Ask the children if they can tell you about something that made them feel angry. Talk about how feelings of anger often build up inside before exploding like a volcano. Can the children suggest what this explosion might look like? For example, shouting, stamping feet, throwing things or hitting out. Suggest ideas and strategies that may help the children control their angry outbursts. (PSE2)

Literacy

- Use simple information books to explain some of the theories about what happened to the dinosaurs when they became extinct 65 million years ago (meteorite impact, volcanic eruptions and climate change). Ask the children if there is anything else they would like to know and use the books to find the answers. (L1)
- Make a word bank of vocabulary to describe volcanic eruptions. Write the words on a flip chart or white board. Keep adding to the list and encourage the children to have a go at adding to the list themselves as well. (L1, 2)

Mathematics

- Provide jugs and funnels for the children to fill clear squeezable bottles with red coloured water. Encourage them to squeeze the bottles so that the 'lava water' overflows. Use mathematical language to talk about filling and emptying the bottles. (M2)
- Create lava patterns with cornflour and water paste. Make three bowls of different coloured paste with yellow, red and orange food colouring. Provide syringes and challenge the children to make repeating patterns with the paste. (M2)

Understanding the World

- Show the children how to create a volcanic eruption (see activity opposite). (UW2)
- Read *Volcanoes* by Stephanie Turnbull to find out what volcanoes are and why and how they erupt. Explain that when the dinosaurs were alive there were a lot more active volcanoes than nowadays. Visit http://www.usborne.com/quicklinks/eng to find some video footage of eruptions. (UW2, 3)
- Talk about the impact of a volcanic eruption on the lives of people who live nearby. Explain that when a volcano erupts, ash rains down and covers everything on land and people have to wear face masks to help them breathe. Although lava moves very slowly, it cannot be stopped and destroys towns and villages. Even planes cannot fly through the ash cloud. (UW1)

Expressive Arts and Design

- Make large-scale volcano spatter pictures. Roll out a large piece of paper on the floor outside. Cut out the shape of a volcano from brown sugar paper and stick it on the paper. Invite the children to paint and flick red, yellow and orange poster paint to create an eruptive effect. (EAD1)

- Show the children some video footage of a volcanic eruption. Point out how the sound gradually builds and the earth shakes as the pressure builds up inside the volcano. Talk about the booming sound as the volcano explodes. Listen for the hissing, sizzling sound the lava makes as it creeps down the side of the mountain. Provide a selection of instruments for the children to experiment with and encourage them to emulate the sound of a volcano erupting. (EAD2)

Activity: Prehistoric landscape

Learning opportunity: Move confidently in a range of ways, safely negotiating space.

Early Learning Goal: Physical Development. Moving and handling.

Resources: Furniture and large climbing apparatus; tunnels; benches; tables and chairs; blankets and pegs; rope; netting; explorer costumes; binoculars; cameras; maps; tent; camping equipment; clipboards, pencils and paper.

Key vocabulary: Explore, search, dinosaur names, quiet, sneak, climb, over, under, through.

Organisation: Whole group – inviting those who are interested to join the play.

What to do: Create a prehistoric landscape for the children to navigate as dinosaur explorers. Use climbing apparatus and benches to create hills; make tunnels and caves by draping blankets over tables; pretend slides are waterfalls or volcano lava tracks; hang vines made of strips of hessian with paper leaves attached; place pot plants and large rocks in between and around the apparatus.

Provide costumes, explorer and camping equipment, as well as clipboards, paper and pencils to draw maps and write notes.

Step back and allow the children to explore the landscape in search of dinosaurs. Observe and listen, and provide additional resources that may enhance their play.

Activity: Volcanic eruption

Learning opportunity: Talks about why things happen and how things work.

Early Learning Goal: Understanding the world. The world.

Resources: Clay; small plastic bottles; bicarbonate of soda; vinegar; red and orange powder paint; funnels; small bowls; small spoon; syringes or pipettes.

Key vocabulary: Volcano, erupt, explode, react, fizz, bubble, colour, red, orange.

Organisation: Small groups.

What to do: Give each child a small plastic bottle and a lump of clay. They should mould the clay around the bottle into the shape of a volcano, ensuring the bottle opening is unobstructed.

Give each child a small bowl. Pass around some bicarbonate of soda for them to spoon into their bowls. They will need enough to fill their bottles about half full. Pass around some red and orange powder paint for them to mix in. Then give them funnels to pour the mixture into their volcano.

Give each child a syringe or pipette and instruct them to fill it with vinegar. They should then squirt the vinegar into the bottle and watch it erupt. Encourage the children to describe what they can see happening.

Display

Use playground chalks to create a prehistoric landscape mural on a smooth light-coloured outside wall. Draw a rough outline for the children to use as a guide by marking out where the sky and sea are.

Invite the children to draw volcanoes and land, sky and marine dinosaurs on the mural. Provide information books with good quality pictures that they can refer to. Help them to write the name of the dinosaur next to their picture, as well as their own name.

Tip: Crushing up playground chalk and adding a tiny bit of water creates playground paint. The children may find it easier to draw the outline of their dinosaur with a piece of chalk and fill it in with brushes and paint.

Theme 6: Finding fossils

Communication and Language

- Read *Monster Stones: The Story of a Dinosaur Fossil* by Jacqui Bailey and Matthew Lilly to help the children understand how fossilisation occurs.

Physical Development

- Bury miniature dinosaur skeletons in the sand tray and provide small brushes and tweezers for the children to excavate with. (PD1)
- Make dinosaur fossils. Flatten out pieces of air hardening clay and press pasta shapes into them to create pictures of dinosaurs. Remove the pasta pieces to reveal skeletal imprints that look like fossilised remains. (PD1)

Personal, Social and Emotional Development

- Blow up images of dinosaur skeletons to A3 size, paste them onto different coloured card and cut each image into five sections. Hide the pieces around the setting. Divide the children into groups of five. Assign each group a colour and challenge them work together to seek out the pieces and reassemble the skeletons. (PSE1)
- Read *Dinosaurs Love Underpants* by Claire Freedman and Ben Cort. It offers a humorous alternative theory about how dinosaurs became extinct. Pause part-way through and talk about the dinosaurs' behaviour. Do the children have any ideas about might happen if the dinosaurs keep fighting they way they are? (PSE2)

Literacy

- Provide clipboards and pencils for the children to take notes as role-play archaeologists (see role-play archaeological dig activity). Set up a chalk board easel next to the archaeologist's tent with a diagram of the excavation site. Provide chalks for the children to mark their finds and write notes. (L1, 2)

Mathematics

- Count the bones on dinosaur skeletons. (M1)
- Cut out some cardboard bones and challenge the children to make shapes out of them. (M2)

Understanding the World

- Read *Stone Girl Bone Girl: The Story of Mary Anning* by Laurence Anholt and Sheila Moxley. Pass around some real fossils for the children to examine. (UW2)

Expressive Arts and Design

- Make a 3D dinosaur skeleton (see activity opposite). (EAD1)
- Find an orchestra recital of Camille Saint Saëns' 'Fossils' from 'Carnival of the Animals' online: (www.youtube.com/watch?v=bcAJpsWWuIY&feature=kp). It includes Ogden Nash's poetic introduction read by Sir Roger Moore. Talk about how the music is meant to sound like the clattering of bones. Take the children into an open space, play the music and encourage them to dance like jangling dinosaur skeletons. (EAD2)
- Set up a role-play museum and archaeological dig (see activity opposite). (EAD2)

Activity: Making a dinosaur skeleton

Learning opportunity: Constructs with a purpose in mind, using a variety of resources.

Early Learning Goal: Expressive Arts and Design. Exploring media and materials.

Resources: Toilet and kitchen roll tubes; strips of newspaper; stiff wire and wire cutters; cellotape or staplers; art roc or Modroc Plaster of Paris strips, or papier mâché powder; pointed scissors; yellow and white poster paints.

Key vocabulary: Skeleton, bones, claws, skull, legs, ribs, bend, join, mould, shape.

Organisation: Small groups, each taking a turn to build a different part of the model.

What to do: Look closely at a picture of a dinosaur skeleton with the children. Talk about the different shapes and sizes of the bones. Can the children identify which dinosaur the skeleton belongs to? Provide some books for them to work it out.

Make large bones by stuffing toilet and kitchen paper tubes with scrunched up newspaper. Join the bones together by pushing strong stiff wire through the tubes, then bend them into shape. Add smaller bones and claws made out of twisted newspaper and staple or cellotape these on.

Cover a balloon in Modelling Rock (Modroc) Plaster of Paris strips or newspaper strips coated in papier mâché paste. When dry, use pointed scissors to cut out the shape of an open mouth, as well as eye sockets. Fix the skull to the model.

Cover the whole skeleton in Modroc or papier mâché to strengthen it. When dry, paint the entire model off-white.

Safety note: If you are happy to allow the children to use the wire cutters, ensure they are under very close supervision and the cutters are moved away after each use.

Activity: Role-play museum and archaeological dig

Learning opportunity: Engages in imaginative role play.

Early Learning Goal: Expressive Arts and Design.
Being imaginative.

Resources: Indoor museum: Large dinosaur skeletons; dinosaur pictures and posters; display boxes (open shoe boxes and empty aquarium tanks will do); signs; labels; coloured card; pens; leaflets; scissors; pens; hole punches; dinosaur stampers; till and money.

Outdoor archaeological dig: Large sand tray, sand pit or area of soil; sieves; hammers; chisels; brushes; cameras; binoculars; magnifying glasses; fossils; dinosaur skeletons; broken pottery (with smoothed edges); tent (a piece of rope and a blanket will do the trick); small zip-lock plastic bags; sticky labels; information books.

Key vocabulary: Museum, exhibit, artefact, display, information, ticket, archaeologist , palaeontologist, excavate, fossil, bone, hammer, chisel, brush, dig, uncover, scrape, brush, clean, chip.

Organisation: Whole group – inviting those who are interested to join the play.

What to do: Ask the children to help you set up a role-play dinosaur museum. Ask them what will be needed and make a list of items. Set up a ticket desk, platforms/cases for displaying exhibits. Make signs and labels. Give the children coloured card, scissors and pens to make tickets and hole punches or dinosaur stampers for stamping them.

Meanwhile, set up an archaeological dig outside. Either use a large sand tray or bury dinosaur skeletons, skulls, fossils and pottery pieces in a sand pit or soiled area. Erect a tent nearby and put excavation tools, magnifiers and cameras inside.

Explain to the children that the area has been designated 'an area of special interest' because dinosaur fossils have been found in the past. Step back and allow them to start a fossil hunt. As fossils and skeletons are discovered, provide information books for the children to identify their finds. They might then like to take their fossils to the museum.

Display

Use the dinosaur skeleton the children have made as an exhibit for the role-play museum. Ask the children what kind of dinosaur it was and use books to find out some information about it. Help them to put together some short information cards containing key facts. Encourage the children to write their own labels to stick onto the skeleton.

Bringing it all together

Creating a 'Prehistoric play landscape'

Work together to create a small world prehistoric landscape that the children can use as a backdrop for imaginative play.

Preparation

Find a large wooden board (a thin piece of medium-density fibreboard (MDF) is fine). If possible, it is a nice idea to cut the board into an irregular shape so it looks like an island. Then sand the edges to smooth them off.

Gather the children and explain that you would like to make a small world prehistoric landscape that they can use when playing with toy dinosaurs. Look at pictures in information books and talk about the features of a prehistoric landscape, for instance, mountains, volcanoes, rivers, desserts, large plants and forests.

Explain that the landscape is going to be junk modelled. Ask the children to think about what kinds of objects they can use to represent different shapes on the landscape. For example, yoghurt pots for mountains and volcanoes, margarine tub lids for lakes and kitchen rolls cut in half for rivers. Ask the children to bring in from home any junk that they think might be useful.

Make the base

Bring the children to the wooden board in small groups. Invite them to suggest ideas about the design of the landscape. Provide PVA glue so that they can stick junk objects onto the board and create the basic lay of the land.

Provide Modroc or Plaster of Paris strips and ask the children to cover the entire base. Leave it to go hard.

Add the detail

Gather the children around the base. Encourage them to point out the different features and talk about what each is meant to be. Ask them for suggestions about how the features can be made more recognisable; with paint, for example. Can the children suggest any art and craft materials that might create a good effect?

Working in small groups, ask the children to decorate the base. Provide poster paint for basic colour, blue cellophane and glitter for water, real sand for dessert regions, real stones for rocks and green felt for foliage.

When the model is complete, give it a coat of watered down PVA glue to make it more hard wearing.

Play

Put the playscape in a prominent position for the children to play with. Ask them how they feel about it. Is there anything they have forgotten? Is there anything they would do differently next time?

Resources

All books were available from leading booksellers at the time of writing

Resources to collect

- Many museums have collections of real fossils that they lend out to schools.
- Dinosaur scene kits and replica dinosaur skulls/fossils
- Small and large toy dinosaurs, a tuff spot play surface
- Dinosaur puppets, toys and crafts
- Small world scenes with volcanoes and explorers
- Numbered dinosaur footprints and excavation kits
- Dinosaur weaving frames, wooden templates
- Dinosaur ice-cube trays, silicone moulds/polymer clay
- Wooden magnetic dinosaur construction sets.

Everyday resources

- Junk modelling materials; boxes, packaging, toilet and kitchen roll tubes, plastic tubs, newspaper
- Strong, stiff wire and wire cutters; flat wooden board
- Cellotape, staplers, pointed scissors, glue, sticky labels, hole punches
- Art roc or Modroc Plaster of Paris strips, or papier mâché powder; air hardening clay; plaster of paris
- Paint brushes and poster/powder paints
- Coloured card, paper, clipboards, pens, pencils
- Easel with chalk board, chalks and board rubbers
- Zip-lock plastic bags, wire/plastic coat hangers, bicarbonate of soda, vinegar, red food colouring, squeezy bottles, cornflour, food colouring
- Tent or rope and blanket
- Musical instruments
- Jugs, funnels, syringes, pipettes.

Information books

- *Monster Stones: The Story of a Dinosaur Fossil* by Jacqui Bailey and Matthew Lilly
- *My First Book of Dinosaurs* by Dougal Dixon and Dee Phillips
- *Fossil* by Claire Ewart
- *Big Book of Big Dinosaurs* by Alex Frith and Fabiano Fiorin
- *DK First Facts: Dinosaurs* by Charlie Gardener
- *Usborne Naturetrail: Rocks and Fossils* by Struan Reid
- *Usborne First Encyclopedia of Dinosaurs and Prehistoric Life* by Sam Taplin
- *Volcanoes* by Stephanie Turnbull.

Story books

- *Dinosaurs Galore!* by Giles Andreae and David Wojtowycz *Dinosaur Dig!*, *Dinosaur Rescue!* and *Dinosaur Zoom!* by Penny Dale
- *Gigantosaurus* by Jonny Duddle
- *Never Ask a Dinosaur to Dinner* by Gareth Edwards and Guy Parker-Rees
- *Dinosaurs Love Underpants* by Claire Freedman and Ben Cort
- *Can I Bring My Pterodactyl to School, Ms. Johnson?* by Lois G. Grambling and Judy Love
- *Katie and the Dinosaurs* by James Mayhew
- *Bumpus Jumpus Dinosaurumpus* by Tony Mitton and Guy Parker-Rees
- *Dinosaurs Have Feelings series* by Brian Moses and Mike Gordon
- *Linus the Vegetarian T. Rex* by Robert Neubecker
- *Ten Terrible Dinosaurs* by Paul Stickland
- *The Super Swooper Dinosaur* by Martin Waddell and Leonie Ward
- *How Do Dinosaurs...* series by Jane Yolen and Mark Teague.

Websites

- Natural History Museum: www.nhm.ac.uk
- Lyme Regis Fossil Festival: www.fossilfestival.co.uk
- BBC Nature: www.bbc.co.uk/nature/prehistoric
- CBeebies: Andy's Dinosaur Adventures: www.bbc.co.uk/cbeebies/andys-dinosaur-adventures

Early years dinosaur resources and toys

- www.reflectionsonlearning.co.uk
- www.arc-education.co.uk
- www.tts-group.co.uk
- www.earlyyearsresources.co.uk
- www.cosydirect.com
- www.yellow-door.net

Poems and rhymes

- *Dinosaur Poems* by John Foster and Korky Paul
- *Stomp, Chomp, Big Roars! Here Come the Dinosaurs!* by Kaye Umansky and Nick Sharratt.

Resources for planning

- **England:** Department for Education (2014) 'Statutory Framework for the Early Years Foundation Stage' (www.foundationyears.org.uk/eyfs-statutory-framework/)
- **Northern Ireland:** CCEA (2011) 'Northern Ireland Curriculum' (www.nicurriculum.org.uk/foundation_stage/)
- **Scotland:** The Scottish Government (2008) 'Curriculum for Excellence' (www.educationscotland.gov.uk/earlyyears/curriculum/index.asp)
- **Wales:** Welsh Government (2008) 'Framework for children's learning for 3 to 7 year olds in Wales' (http://learning.wales.gov.uk/resources/framework-for-childrens-learning/?skip=1&lang=en).

Collecting evidence of children's learning

Monitoring children's development is an important task. Making a profile of children's achievements, strengths, capabilities interests and learning will help you to see progress and will draw attention to those who are having difficulties for some reason. If a child needs additional professional help, such as speech therapy, these cumulative profiles will provide valuable evidence.

Profiles should cover all the Areas of Learning, as defined by the relevant UK framework, and be the result of collaboration between practitioners, parents and carers. Parents should be made aware of your record keeping policies when their child joins your group. Show parents the types of documentation that you are keeping and make sure they understand their purpose. As a general rule, documentation should be open. Families should have access to their child's documentation at any time and know they can contribute to it. Take regular opportunities to talk to parents about children's progress. If you have formal discussions regarding children about whom you have particular concerns, a dated record of the main points should be kept.

Keeping it manageable

Documentation should be helpful in informing practitioners, adult helpers and parents and always be for the benefit of the child. The golden rule is to keep it simple, manageable and useful. Do not try to make records following every activity!

Documentation will basically fall into two categories – observations and reflections:

Observations

- **Spontaneous observations:** Sometimes you will want to make a note of observations as they happen e.g. a child is heard counting cars accurately during a play activity, or is seen to play collaboratively for the first time.
- **Planned observations:** Sometimes you will plan to make observations of children's developing skills within a planned activity. Using the learning opportunity identified for an activity will help you to make appropriate judgments about children's capabilities, strengths and interests, and to record them systematically.

To collect information:

- Talk to children about their activities and listen to their responses.
- Listen to children talking to each other.
- Observe children's work such as early writing, drawings, paintings and models. (Keeping photocopies or photographs can be useful in tracking progress. Photographs are particularly useful to monitor children's development in the outdoor environment.)

Sometimes it may be appropriate to set up 'one off' activities for the purposes of monitoring development. Some groups at the beginning of each term, for example, ask children to write their name and to make a drawing of themselves to record their progressing skills in both co-ordination and observation.

Reflections

It is useful to spend regular time reflecting on the children's progress. Aim to make some comments about each child each week, and discuss these regularly with colleagues and families.

Informing your planning

Collecting evidence about children's progress is time consuming and it is important that it is useful. When planning, use the information collected to help you to decide what learning opportunities you need to provide next for each child. For example, a child who has poor pencil or brush control will benefit from more play with dough or construction toys to build strength of muscles in the hands and fingers.

Example observation sheet

Name: Lucy Field

Date: 17.1.13

Area of Learning: Mathematics. Count reliably with numbers from 1 to 20.

Context (Please tick):

Child-initiated: √ **Adult-led:**
Alone: **In a group:** √

Observation: Lucy is playing outside with two friends. She is trying to build the tallest tower and counting the bricks. "1, 2, 3, 4, 5, 7, 8. Mine's 8. Yours is only 7." She knocks the tower down, chuckles and starts to build again, counting as she places the bricks. "1, 2, 3, 4, 5, 7." The tower falls over. "Oh blow. I wanted to do 20."

What next: Check Lucy knows 6 follows 5. Encourage use of the outdoor counting grids, skittles and number rhyme CD.

Observer: E. M. Hogg

Overview of areas covered through 'Dinosaurs'

	Communication and Language	Physical Development	Personal, Social and Emotional Development	Literacy	Mathematics	Understanding the World	Expressive Arts and Design
Meat-eating predators	Listening and attention Understanding Speaking	Moving and handling Health and self-care	Self-confidence and self-awareness Managing feelings and behaviour Making relationships	Reading Writing	Numbers Shape, space and measures	People and communities The world Technology	Exploring and using media and materials Being imaginative
Gentle giants	Listening and attention Understanding Speaking	Moving and handling Health and self-care	Self-confidence and self-awareness Managing feelings and behaviour Making relationships	Reading Writing	Numbers Shape, space and measures	People and communities The world Technology	Exploring and using media and materials Being imaginative
Dinosaurs in the sky	Listening and attention Understanding Speaking	Moving and handling Health and self-care	Self-confidence and self-awareness Managing feelings and behaviour Making relationships	Reading Writing	Numbers Shape, space and measures	People and communities The world Technology	Exploring and using media and materials Being imaginative
Dinosaurs of the deep	Listening and attention Understanding Speaking	Moving and handling Health and self-care	Self-confidence and self-awareness Managing feelings and behaviour Making relationships	Reading Writing	Numbers Shape, space and measures	People and communities The world Technology	Exploring and using media and materials Being imaginative
Explosive landscape	Listening and attention Understanding Speaking	Moving and handling Health and self-care	Self-confidence and self-awareness Managing feelings and behaviour Making relationships	Reading Writing	Numbers Shape, space and measures	People and communities The world Technology	Exploring and using media and materials Being imaginative
Finding fossils	Listening and attention Understanding Speaking	Moving and handling Health and self-care	Self-confidence and self-awareness Managing feelings and behaviour Making relationships	Reading Writing	Numbers Shape, space and measures	People and communities The world Technology	Exploring and using media and materials Being imaginative

Note: For each theme, highlight the Early Learning Goal areas covered through both adult focused and child-initiated activities relating to 'Dinosaurs'.

Home links

The theme of 'Dinosaurs' lends itself to useful links with children's homes and families. Through working together, children and adults gain respect for each other and build comfortable and confident relationships.

Establishing partnerships

- Keep parents informed about the themes for 'Dinosaurs' and the activities for each week. By understanding the work of the group, parents can get involved by contributing ideas, time and resources.
- Photocopy the 'Family page' for each child to take home.
- Invite children to bring in toy dinosaurs and books about dinosaurs from home.
- Find out what museums, exhibitions and archaeological sites there are in your local area. Put this information on a fact sheet and hand it out to parents to give them ideas about places they can take their children to learn more about prehistoric life.
- Send home a large cuddly toy dinosaur for the children to take on an adventure. Explain this can be a real adventure, a day out for example, or an imaginary adventure made up by the child and their family. Send a note book home for parents to record the adventure story.
- Lend out dinosaur stories for children to share with their parents at home.

Visiting enthusiasts

- Find out if there is an education officer at a local museum who is willing to visit and bring in some prehistoric objects for the children to see.
- Invite vegetarian families to bring in a vegetarian dish. Ask them to tell everyone about the type of food they eat and the reasons why they choose to be vegetarian.
- Find out if any of the children own a pet reptile that they can bring in to the setting. Otherwise, invite an education officer from a local zoo or wildlife park to bring some reptiles in.

Resource requests

- Ask parents to contribute clean food and household packaging that the children can use for junk modelling.
- Find out if any parents have interesting prehistoric items such as fossils that they can send in from home.